Great Mysteries

HOUDINI

by Laura Alden
illustrated by Betty Raskin

Created by

THE CHILD'S WORLD

Distributed by **CHILDRENS PRESS®**
Chicago, Illinois

cover photograph courtesy of Historical Pictures Service, Chicago
cover design by Kathryn Schoenick

CHILDRENS PRESS HARDCOVER EDITION
ISBN 0-516-06217-4

CHILDRENS PRESS PAPERBACK EDITION
ISBN 0-516-46217-2

Library of Congress Cataloging-in-Publication Data

Alden, Laura, 1955-
    Houdini / by Laura Alden ; illustrated by Betty Raskin.
      p. cm. — (Great mysteries)
    Includes index.
    Summary: A biography of the mysterious magician, focusing on his
great escapes, wondrous illusions, crusade against spiritualism, and
attempt to communicate with his wife after his death.
    ISBN 0-89565-456-3
    1. Houdini, Harry, 1874-1926—Juvenile literature.   2. Magicians—
United States—Biography—Juvenile literature.   [1. Houdini,
Harry, 1874-1926.   2. Magicians.]   I. Raskin, Betty, ill.
II. Title.   III. Series: Great mysteries (Elgin, Ill.)
GV1545.H8A53   1989
793.8′092′4—dc19
[B]   88-34126
[92]   CIP
                                                                     AC

1 2 3 4 5 6 7 8 9 10 11 12 R 97 96 95 94 93 92 91 90 89

Great Mysteries

HOUDINI

for Barry and Joey

CONTENTS

Man of Mystery 7

Great Escapes 27

Mysterious Illusions 45

The Great Mystery .55

Last Challenge 71

The Mystery of Magic 89

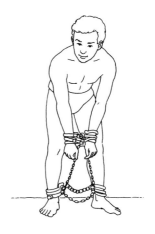

Chapter 1

Man of Mystery

You're sitting in a darkened room with a crowd of people, waiting. Suddenly, a mysterious man in a black cape appears. He removes his black, silk hat and shows you it's empty. Then he reaches inside. Out comes a large, white rabbit. Next he pulls a coin from thin air. With a snap of his fingers, it disappears and then reappears in a glass box across the stage.

A young, female assistant steps out onto the stage. With a wave of his wand, the magician makes the woman disappear. With an abracadabra, he brings her back—and saws her in half! You sit holding your breath as he's locked into a large trunk, and then sigh with relief as he escapes with ease.

You may know there's a trick behind everything he does, but you're still struck with the wonder of magic!

Magic and Magicians

Poof! Shazam! Abracadabra! As long as there have been people, there have been magicians. They've come in all shapes and sizes. Some makers of magic have used their skills to help and to entertain. Some (especially long ago) have used magic to gain control over others.

To early humans, everything was magic. Thunder and lightning, the sun and the stars, birth and death—all were fearful and mysterious. When people didn't understand something that happened, they believed it must have been caused by magic. Those who learned how to make "impossible" things happen gained power.

There were those who deliberately set out to become magicians. Some of them really believed in the super-natural; some were looking for a way to cheat people. They might brew you some "magical" chamomile tea for your cold and then read your future in the tea leaves.

There were some who became magicians by accident. They studied nature and learned to predict when it would rain or when it would grow cold. They studied herbs and other plants and learned how to grow food better or how to heal diseases. People were amazed at their abilities and thought they must have supernatural powers.

As human knowledge has grown, people have believed less in the power of wands and words. Today magic has become less scary and more fun! Magicians have learned to be tricksters and actors. And today they admit it too.

The element of mystery, though, has never left the prac-tice of magic. And one of the most mysterious magicians ever to live was a man named Harry Houdini.

The Great Houdini

Now, Harry Houdini was a real person. That is one fact we know for certain. But the rest of Houdini's life story is full of mysteries. Perhaps that is why, more than sixty years after his death, Houdini still ranks as the most famous magician who ever lived.

There are good reasons, amazing reasons, for Houdini's fame. No handcuffs, rope, or jail could hold him. He escaped from bolted crates and coffins that had been lowered underwater. He even found his way out of the chained-up carcass of an embalmed sea monster!

Today, we still wonder at much of Harry Houdini's magic. The legends surrounding him have grown like Pinocchio's nose. He remains a true mystery.

Two Names and Two Birthdays

Houdini always said he was born in Appleton, Wisconsin, on April 6, 1874. But others say he wasn't born in Wisconsin—or on April 6. They say his name wasn't Harry or Houdini either!

It is true that Houdini's parents, Samuel and Cecilia Weiss, brought their large family to America from Hungary in 1874. Samuel, a rabbi, had been offered a job with a new Jewish congregation in Appleton, Wisconsin. It is also true that *sometime* in 1874, Cecilia gave birth to a son.

But from records in Hungary, researchers have discovered part of the answer to the mystery of Houdini's birth. They say Samuel and Cecilia's son was born in Budapest, Hungary, not in Wisconsin. The date of his birth, because of a mistake in the calendar, may have been recorded as March 24, not April 6. Only Houdini's parents knew the real date.

The mystery baby's name was Ehrich Weiss. He changed it to Harry Houdini when he began his show-business career. He had two names and two birthdays—a perfect trick for a master mystifier!

The Young Magician

Ehrie, as he was called, began doing magic when he was very young. He let his friends tie his wrists together behind his back. Presto! He was free in minutes!

According to legend, Ehrie made his first public appearance on the trapeze at the age of nine. He applied to Jack Hoefler's Five Cent Circus and was hired as "Ehrich, the Prince of the Air." He performed in red woolen underwear and received thirty-five cents a week. He "flew through the air with the greatest of ease" on the trapeze and then did a variation of an old trick, bending over backwards and picking things up with the mouth. Only Ehrie bent over backwards and picked things up with his eyelids! He loved the applause and vowed to become a real performer.

Ehrie also became fascinated with locks at an early age. He spent a lot of time with the town locksmith. There, he learned how to pick every lock in the shop. Soon after, he demonstrated that he could pick every lock in the town. One night, Ehrie unlocked the front doors of all the stores in downtown Appleton! The people there still talk about that!

Ehrie's mother soon noticed her son's skill with locks. Pieces of apple dessert kept disappearing from the cupboard. So, Mrs. Weiss put a lock on the cupboard. The apple dessert still kept disappearing. Then, she padlocked the cupboard door. Poof! This time the whole pie was gone! Mrs. Weiss realized that Ehrie's ability to pick locks was more than just a hobby. No pie was safe!

"Shake me—I'm Magic"

When Ehrie was thirteen, the Weiss family moved to New York. The family had never had much money, and Ehrie's father hoped to start a small, religious school there. But he became ill and could not work very much. Ehrie found jobs or made up ways to make money. Once he pinned a card to his hat. It read:

Christmas is coming
Turkeys are fat
Please drop a quarter
In the Messenger Boy's hat

People passing by did just that. Before Ehrie returned home, he hid coins up his sleeves, in his hair, and behind his ears. When his mother opened the door, Ehrie commanded, "Shake me—I'm magic!"

As she shook him, the hidden coins showered onto the floor. It did seem like magic.

The Beginning

Ehrie's first magic trick came from his brother Theo's boss. Theo's boss taught Theo a simple coin trick, and Theo, in turn, taught it to Ehrie. In Ehrie's quick hands, the quarter's disappearance really did seem like magic. The two boys began talking and reading about magic and practicing magic tricks as often as they could.

To earn money for his family, Ehrie took a job as a necktie cutter in a factory. He got the job through a trick, of course! He walked into the factory office and took the "Help Wanted" sign out of the window.

"Someone has been hired," he told those who were waiting for an interview. "Thank you for waiting."

At the factory Ehrie met Jacob Hyman, who was also interested in magic. During lunches, they talked magic and practiced tricks. But magic was still just a hobby for Ehrie, until one day Ehrie read a book about the great French magician, Jean-Eugene Robert-Houdin. Suddenly, Ehrie knew what he wanted to do with his life. He wanted to be a "maker of miracles," just like Robert-Houdin. And that's when Ehrich Weiss became Harry Houdini.

The Houdini Brothers

Harry Houdini began his professional magic career at the age of seventeen. He teamed with his brother Theo, and "The Houdini Brothers" set out to become magicians.

At first, Harry and Theo gave shows at parties, club meetings, and beer halls. Abracadabra! Harry produced a flower through a buttonhole of his jacket. Shazam! A coin disappeared from Theo's fingertips.

The Houdini Brothers saved their best trick for last. First, Harry tied Theo's hands behind his back. Then, Harry led Theo to a large trunk. Theo got in, and Harry closed and locked the lid. For extra security, Harry then tied a rope around the trunk. Last, Harry put a screen in front of the trunk.

"When I clap my hands three times," Harry said, "behold, a miracle!"

Harry stepped behind the screen and clapped his hands three times. Immediately, Theo stepped out in front! Then, Theo quickly moved the screen to one side. Harry wasn't behind it! Theo untied and unlocked the trunk and lifted the lid. Harry climbed out! The audience cheered when they saw Harry's hands tied behind his back, just as Theo's had been.

This trick, called Metamorphosis, was one Houdini would do throughout his whole life. It was a puzzling trick. For some, it really did seem to be a "miracle."

Slowly, the Houdini Brothers became better and better known. They even took their act to the Chicago World's Fair in 1893. At the fair, they saw other acts—fire eaters,

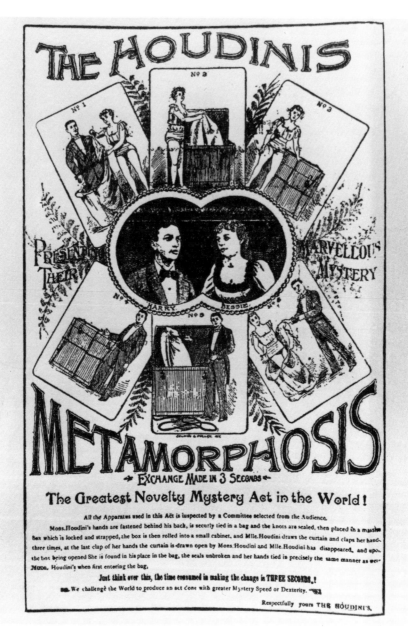

Houdini advertises his new act and his new partner. (courtesy Historical Pictures Service, Chicago)

sword swallowers, and belly dancers. They also saw a performer escape from a pair of handcuffs. Harry, who loved escapes, began to practice the handcuff trick.

The most impressive trick Harry saw at the fair was done by a Hindu conjurer. The East Indian swallowed a dozen needles and some cotton. Then he opened his mouth and pulled out the needles. But now they were threaded! Harry remembered this trick and would later do it himself. He may have even gotten the secret from the mysterious East Indian at the Chicago World's Fair.

Bess

The next summer, Harry and Theo performed on Coney Island in New York. There, Harry met a young woman who was part of a song and dance act. Wilhelmina Beatrice Rahner, "Bess," was a tiny woman with dark hair. Harry fell in love with her. Two weeks later, the eighteen-year-old Bess and twenty-year-old Harry were married.

Bess became not only Harry's wife, but also his new business partner. She replaced Theo in the act, and she soon learned how hard her new husband worked to produce his magic. Houdini slept only five hours a night. The rest of the time he spent exercising or practicing with ropes and handcuffs. He also "played" with coins and cards to keep his fingers—and toes!—limber.

Dr. Hill's California Concert Company

For several years, the Houdinis crisscrossed the country. They performed in dime museums, traveling circuses,

and with other magicians. At one point, Harry and Bess worked for Dr. Hill's California Concert Company. Dr. Hill sold medicine to people in small towns. (The medicine probably never cured anyone of anything. People didn't know that Dr. Hill mixed it up himself.)

The Houdinis gathered a crowd for Dr. Hill by doing their magic act. Then he would sell his "magic" elixir.

One day Dr. Hill asked Harry to add another trick to his

act. He wanted to attract more people to the show. "You are now a spiritualist," he told Harry.

Harry knew that spiritualists believed they could communicate with the dead. Some spiritualists, called "mediums," passed messages from the dead to the living. Houdini also knew that most spiritualists only pretended to receive these messages. But he and Bess needed the work. So Harry learned the tricks of spiritualism.

Houdini quickly gained a reputation for his amazing predictions. One night he called a woman's name. The woman was present and stood up. Harry told the woman he had a message from the spirits for her.

"I see a boy on a bicycle," he said. "He is going too fast. He can't stop! Oh, no! He has crashed! His arm may be broken."

The next day the woman's son really did crash on his bicycle and break his arm! Everyone believed it was magic. How else could Houdini have known what was going to happen?

Well, earlier that day, Houdini had seen a boy riding recklessly on his bicycle. He had also seen the boy's mother scolding her son. Houdini discovered the mother's name, and he took a chance. He didn't say when the accident would happen, and he only said the arm might be broken. It was just good luck for Houdini that it came true—though it was bad luck for the boy!

Houdini's new act convinced people that he really had magical powers. He told audiences all about their lives, and what he said was usually exactly right. That was because his "messages from the dead" came from his own research and observations. Sometimes he posed as a Bible salesman. That way he could get a look at family records in old Bibles. He also visited graveyards and read what was on the tombstones and spent time talking to people about their neighbors.

Gradually, though, Houdini began to dislike this part of his job. He didn't believe in spiritualism. He didn't want people to believe he had special powers. Houdini just

(courtesy Historical Pictures Service, Chicago)

wanted to be a magician who knew how to fool people who knew they were being fooled! He didn't want to lie to people.

So, in 1896, Harry and Bess headed back to New York. There was to be much more magic in their lives, but no more lies.

Harry Houdini, Magician

Harry Houdini was not a big man. He stood five feet, eight inches tall. But he looked larger than life on stage. He sounded like a man in control too. Even though there were no microphones during most of Houdini's career, crowds could always hear him.

There was a trick behind every bit of magic Houdini did. But it was a rare person who could figure out what that trick was. Many people have claimed that Houdini must have been able to dematerialize in order to escape from some of the places he escaped from. Others said that he could make objects really vanish or appear. Houdini just laughed at all this and smiled mysteriously. Anyone could do what he did, he said—if they knew how!

This book describes the magic of Harry Houdini. The fact that he used tricks to create his illusions doesn't take away from the fact that he performed some amazing magic.

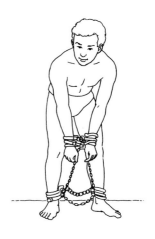

Chapter 2

Great Escapes

Harry Houdini was best known as an escape artist. He escaped from handcuffs, jails, cans, crates, and straitjackets. "I have," he said once, "extricated myself from approximately 12,500 straitjackets, and picked, roughly, 8,300 locks."

Houdini delighted in unusual, impossible escapes. In Chicago he escaped from a huge, sealed envelope —without breaking the paper. In Los Angeles, he got out of a laced U.S. government mail pouch. In Philadelphia, college football players wound a brass chain around a giant football with Houdini inside. The magician was out in thirty-five minutes. Houdini even escaped from the inside of a locked steel vault!

Master Jailbreaker

Early in his career, Houdini learned that spectacular escapes gained him a lot of publicity. Once while he was performing in Chicago, he called some reporters and asked them to meet him at the Chicago Police Department headquarters. He promised them a big story.

A top police official locked Houdini in leg irons and handcuffs and then locked him in a cell. Houdini was free in minutes, but the reporters were unimpressed. They thought he had gotten spare keys. Houdini stripped off all his clothes and challenged them to search him and then lock him up again. They did. They even taped his mouth closed and locked his clothes in a separate cell. In ten minutes Houdini strolled in, fully clothed, from the street!

This time the reporters were impressed. The next day the Chicago *Journal* carried a front-page story about Harry Houdini, who "escaped out of all their handcuffs, leg irons, insane restraints, belts and straitjackets." It was an exaggeration, but Houdini didn't care.

From then on, often, the first thing Houdini did when he got into town was to call the press and go to the police station. He escaped from jails all across the country. People began to believe that Houdini really could escape from anything.

Escapes Around the World

Houdini performed his act around the world. And everywhere, audiences were amazed by his magic.

In England, Houdini stumped the police at the famous Scotland Yard by escaping from their handcuffs. The Lon-

No jail could hold Houdini. (courtesy Historical Pictures Service, Chicago)

29

don police asked Houdini not to reveal how little time it took for him to open their jail cells. Houdini agreed not to. "It made their cells look too easy," he said.

One night in London, a man named the Great Cirnoc stood up in the audience. He said that he, not Houdini, was the one who could escape from any handcuffs.

Houdini was not upset. He challenged the Great Cirnoc to come up on stage and escape from a pair of cuffs he used in his act. First Houdini was locked in the cuffs. He escaped easily, in a few seconds. Then it was the Great Cirnoc's turn. Houdini locked him in the cuffs and even gave him the key, knowing that Cirnoc couldn't reach the lock while in the cuffs.

When a river wasn't available, Houdini used a swimming pool. (courtesy United Press International)

The Great Cirnoc twisted and turned, trying to escape. Finally, he gave up and asked Houdini to let him out. Houdini did while the audience applauded.

Everywhere he went, Houdini's escapes got attention. In Holland, Houdini was tied to the arm of a windmill. His plan was to escape while the windmill turned. But as the giant windmill turned, the arm snapped in half. Houdini crashed to the ground! Miraculously, he was not seriously hurt. The trick had not worked, but the Dutch loved this crazy foreigner who tied himself to windmills!

In Germany, Houdini did something different to get attention. After being handcuffed and tied with chains, he jumped off a bridge and freed himself under water! As he got out of the water, the police arrested him—for walking on the grass! They didn't try to handcuff him, though. It wouldn't have done any good!

Houdini became a star throughout Europe. Carpenters built special escape-proof crates and challenged him to get out. Audiences crowded theatres to see Houdini win every challenge. They loved this mystery man from America.

Houdini traveled around the world—even to Australia. In Melbourne, Houdini was handcuffed and chained on a bridge over the Yarra River. He leaped into the water, and then a dead body floated to the surface! People screamed. They thought it was Houdini. But then Houdini popped to the surface. The body had probably been caught under water and Houdini's splash released it. No one knew who the body was—mysteries just seemed to follow Houdini!

Musical Cells

In January of 1906, Houdini cased the United States Jail in Washington, D.C. There was a famous jail cell there. The cell had once held Charles Guiteau, the man who shot and killed President James A. Garfield. The door of the cell sank down into a three-foot brick wall. It could only be opened with a special key.

Houdini talked the warden into locking him, once again naked, into Guiteau's cell. He was out in two minutes! So he decided to have some fun. While the warden and the

newspaper reporters sipped coffee in the warden's office, Houdini opened the cell doors of the other prisoners! He instructed the surprised inmates to switch cells and then he locked them up again! Then Houdini marched into the warden's office, just twenty-two minutes after he'd been locked up.

His escape—and the game of musical cells—amazed the reporters. This time Houdini didn't just make the local papers. He was "big news" all across the country!

Underwater Wonders

When people became bored with jail escapes, Houdini advertised a new trick. It would be a "death-defying mystery," the advertisements said. If he failed to escape, he would face "a drowning death."

On January 27, 1908, Houdini strode to the front of the stage of the Columbia Theatre in St. Louis, Missouri. "Ladies and Gentlemen," he began, "my latest invention—The Milk Can. I will be placed in this can, and it will be filled with water. A committee from the audience will lock the padlocks and place the keys down in the footlights. I will attempt to escape. If I should fail to appear, my assistants will smash the Milk Can and do everything possible to save my life."

Dressed in his bathing suit, the magician stepped up to the Milk Can. He wedged his body down into the airtight, metal can. It looked like the milk cans used by dairy farmers. It had been made larger, though, to hold a person. As Houdini climbed in, water sloshed over the sides of the can. More water was added to fill the can to the top. Then, Houdini was locked inside. The curtain was drawn in front of the Milk Can.

Onlookers held their breath. After thirty seconds, they gasped for air. How could Houdini survive? More time passed. Ninety seconds. Two minutes. He must be drowning! Two-and-a-half minutes—*three minutes!*

"Save him!" someone screamed. Houdini's helper raised an axe.

Just then, a dripping Houdini stepped out from behind the curtain. The audience rose to its feet. People shouted with relief and clapped with wonder. There was the Milk Can—still padlocked. The Great Houdini defied the laws of nature!

From then on, Houdini included water escapes in his show. The danger of death fascinated his fans. Houdini made sure there was really very little danger. He practiced holding his breath until he could hold it for almost four minutes. And how did he get out of the can? Only Houdini knew for sure.

The Chinese Water Torture Cell

Houdini's best known water escape was called the Chinese Water Torture Cell. He also called it the U.S.D. (for "upside down"). Houdini presented this escape for the first time in Berlin, Germany, in 1912.

Once again, Houdini announced that he would perform a death-defying feat. A special glass-sided cell was built for him with a set of stocks at the top. One hundred gallons of water was poured into the cell. Houdini was handcuffed and the stocks were fit around his feet. Then ropes lifted and lowered him into the water-filled cell, hanging upside-down. He was then padlocked inside.

The audience saw Houdini hanging there, head down in the water, before the curtain in front of the cell was closed. Just as with the Milk Can escape, the crowd grew nervous as the minutes ticked by. Soon they started to yell. Houdini's assistants raised their axes to smash the glass. Just then Houdini appeared! The Chinese Water Torture Cell was still padlocked. The stunned spectators erupted with cheers.

Poster advertising the Chinese Water Torture Cell (courtesy Historical Pictures Service, Chicago)

Straitjacket Stunts

But the happiness Houdini felt at his success did not last long. In July, his mother, Cecilia, died. To mask the sorrow he felt, Houdini worked harder than ever. His brother, Theo, suggested that he escape from a straitjacket in front of an audience. Always before, he had released himself inside a cabinet or behind a screen. A public escape would be more dramatic. Houdini agreed. He wouldn't be giving away any secrets. The "trick" to the escape was not a magic one. It depended on Houdini's physical strength and his ability to twist and stretch his body.

Houdini also added another touch to the trick. In September, 1914, he asked the Kansas City *Post* to advertise his new escape. The Great Houdini would release himself from a straitjacket—while hanging upside down from the top of the Post Building!

Over 5000 people gathered to see Houdini hang like a ham upside down from the roof of the newspaper building. The police officers told reporters that no one could escape from their straitjacket—not even Houdini.

The newspaper agreed to give Houdini fifteen minutes to try to escape. Then they tied him to a crane and hoisted him thirty feet into the air.

Those who watched from below could hardly believe their eyes! Houdini bent and wrenched his body to get out of the straitjacket. It seemed as if he didn't have any bones! But the crowd didn't have to watch long. In two-and-a-half minutes, Houdini dropped the straitjacket down to the street.

Houdini hangs from a building strapped in a straitjacket. In just a few minutes, he will be free. (courtesy United Press International)

A Close Call

Was there anything Houdini couldn't escape from? Well, there was one occasion when he almost didn't make it.

In 1904, a London newspaper, the *Daily Illustrated Mirror*, challenged Houdini to escape from a pair of special handcuffs. They had been designed to stay locked forever, unless a special key was used. Houdini accepted the challenge.

The key turned, locking the handcuffs on Houdini's wrists. Houdini addressed the audience of 4000 people. "Ladies and gentlemen, I am now locked up in a handcuff that it has taken a British mechanic five years to make. I do not know whether I am going to get out of it or not, but I can assure you I am going to do my best."

The orchestra began to play. Houdini climbed into a cabinet made of curtains. Twenty-two minutes later, he stuck his head and hands out to get a better look at the cuffs. The orchestra played another tune. Thirteen more minutes went by. The handcuffed Houdini stepped out, perspiring, to get a cushion to kneel on. Twenty more minutes passed. (Audiences were more patient in those days.) Houdini came out, put a pocketknife in his teeth, and cut his coat off. The crowd clapped and cheered.

Houdini got back into the cabinet. After ten *more* minutes, he called out for Bess to get him a glass of water. The orchestra struck up again. Suddenly, Houdini bounded from the cabinet, free!

The audience roared. It had taken him over an hour, but Houdini had escaped the inescapable! The crowd carried him around on their shoulders. Houdini wept onstage. Bess wept offstage.

It had been a close call. But Houdini's magic had finally worked—or so everyone thought. To this day, some people think when Bess saw Houdini couldn't get out of the

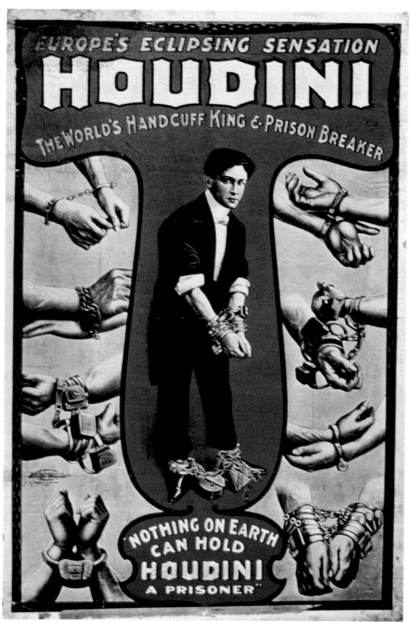

Poster advertising the "Handcuff King" (courtesy Historical Pictures Service, Chicago)

handcuffs, she went to the owner of the handcuffs and pleaded for the key. Then she smuggled the key to Houdini in the glass of water. We don't know if that is true or not—but a quick-thinking wife can be as good as magic!

The Great Escape Artist

Houdini rarely had such close calls. His "magic" was to plan carefully for each escape. He could hide picklocks so that they would not be found no matter how carefully he was searched. He could swallow tools, bring them back up, and then swallow them again! He also had an almost photographic memory for handcuff locks. He said he could cut a key to fit a lock after just a glance at it. Houdini's skill as a magician allowed him to palm keys. He could also misdirect the attention of his searchers. One of his favorite places to hide picklocks was on the soles of his feet. He pasted them there with surgeon's cement. Somehow, people never looked there!

Still, many of Houdini's escapes could not be explained even if he had a key or picklock. That was Houdini's magic!

Chapter 3

Mysterious Illusions

Magicians have made lots of things disappear: coins, glasses of water, articles of clothing. Anything can go when there's a magician around. Magicians are especially fond of making animals disappear: doves, ducks, rabbits, donkeys, and even horses. But no one had ever made an elephant disappear. No one before Houdini, that is.

Bang! Jennie, the 10,000-pound daughter of Jumbo the elephant, vanished into thin air when Houdini fired a pistol. Even Houdini's critics said that was an unbeatable trick.

The magician first had Jennie do a little magic herself. He announced that she would make a lump of sugar disappear. As she ate it, the crowd laughed. But then, Houdini led Jennie into a crate frame hung with curtains. The curtains closed. The cabinet was turned around by a twelve-member stage crew. Houdini fired his pistol. The curtain opened. No elephant. No elephant??? The biggest land animal in the world was nowhere in sight. There was no trap door, no trick backdrop. The five-ton Jennie was simply gone! (And it's not easy to hide an elephant!)

"Crowds will worry themselves to sleep nightly, wondering what Houdini did with his elephant," reported one magazine. So would other magicians.

Said Houdini with a grin, "Even the elephant does not know how it is done!"

Needles

In addition to performing the largest illusion on the magic stage, Houdini could also boast of performing the smallest illusion. He and Bess called the trick "Needles." It came from faraway and mysterious East India.

First, the magician invited a committee of audience members to inspect his mouth to make sure it was empty. Then he would stick out his tongue, lay a handful of needles on it, close his mouth—and swallow the needles! Next, he swallowed a long piece of thread. Making an awful face, Houdini would begin to draw the thread out of his mouth. The crowd gasped! The needles were now threaded on it! A member of the audience committee slowly drew up to a hundred threaded needles out of Houdini's mouth and across the stage. Even the people in the balcony could see the needles gleaming in the stage lights.

Houdini did other small illusions as well. He liked to take off his thumb, wave it, and replace it! Members of a

Houdini and Jennie (courtesy The McManus-Young Collection at the Library of Congress)

committee from the audience saw the stunt from up close. Yet, they couldn't tell how it was done. It really was a trick, of course, but how Houdini did it was a mystery.

Houdini also could cause knots to appear and disappear in a silk scarf. He could push a steel needle through his cheek without drawing blood. Coins would disappear from his fingertips and reappear in a glass box. "The Supreme Ruler of Magic" worked hard to live up to his name!

A Magical Dog

Bess and Harry's life together was enlivened by several pets. Often the birds and animals they took care of had been in Houdini's magic act first. Some of them were talented magicians in their own right!

The Houdinis' little fox terrier, Bobby, could escape

from a pair of miniature handcuffs. He could also wiggle out of a tiny straitjacket. When cards were laid on the floor, Bobby could pick up a card that was called out. Houdini said Bobby was also "the greatest somersault dog that ever lived."

Miss Liberty

Another of the Houdinis' pets helped Houdini do a very special show.

During World War I, Houdini often promoted the American war effort. In one stunt, he put a sheet of glass on top of a table. On top of the glass, he placed a clear fishbowl filled with water. Then he added red and blue liquids to the water and mixed them together. Suddenly—splash!—he plunged his hand into the water and whipped out trails of four-hundred-foot long silk streamers. He unfurled them across the stage, forming several giant American flags.

Before the flags were done waving, Houdini reached into the folds of the banners. He pulled out a live eagle, wings flapping! The wartime audience rose to its feet, shouting and waving. They appreciated Houdini's tribute to their soldier sons. And they loved Houdini's eagle. They called her "Miss Liberty."

Later news stories revealed that Houdini's eagle was a he, not a she. The bird's name originally was Josephus Daniels Abraham Lincoln. No matter. Houdini's eagle still created a special kind of magic when he appeared. Miss Josephus Daniels Abraham Lincoln Liberty was the only tame eagle in the United States.

Walking Through Walls

The elephant and the eagle acts were Houdini originals. But Houdini often bought acts from other magicians. He then added his own touches to them. In London, Houdini purchased the secret to an illusion called "walking through a wall of steel" from an old magician. He changed "the wall of steel" to a wall of bricks—and had it built right on the stage!

As he usually did when starting an illusion, the magician invited a committee made up of twelve audience members to come up onto the stage. The audience committee was assigned the task of watching for any dishonest activity or trick and making sure the magician didn't "cheat." In the brick wall illusion, the audience committee members helped Houdini lay down a seamless cloth rug, which covered most of the stage. Over this they placed a muslin sheet. Houdini told the audience that the rug and sheet would prevent him from using any trap door in the stage floor to go under the wall.

Next Houdini brought out a steel beam, ten feet long and one foot wide, which he placed perpendicular to the audience. On it members of the local bricklayers' union constructed a real brick wall. When they were done, the members of the audience committee stood on the four corners of the rug and two three-fold screens were brought out. The screens were just a little shorter than the wall. They were placed one on each side of the wall, touching the wall so that Houdini couldn't go around it. Now Houdini couldn't go under the wall because of the rug, he couldn't go around the wall because of the

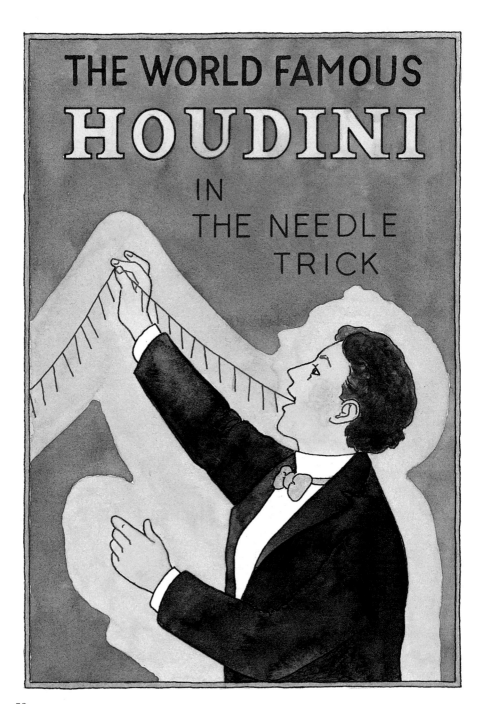

screens, and he couldn't go over the wall because that was in plain sight of the audience. That established, Houdini stepped out of sight behind the screens.

Standing on the right side of the wall, Houdini raised his hands above the screen. "Here I am," he called. There was a drumroll. Houdini shouted, "I'm going. . . . I'm going. . . . I'm gone!" A cymbal crashed and Houdini yelled, "And now, here I am!" There he was on the other side of the brick wall! Once again, the Great Houdini had done the impossible. He had actually walked through a solid brick wall!

How Did He Do It?

How did Houdini work his amazing magic? How could he make things float in the air, pass through solid objects, and appear or disappear at will?

Well, the laws of nature applied to Houdini as much as they do to everyone else. There were tricks behind every illusion Houdini presented. We now know some of the secrets. For instance, we know that Houdini went under that brick wall. There had been a trap door under the covering rug. The rug had enough give to it that Houdini could use his escape skills to slither under the wall. But it doesn't matter that it wasn't "real" magic. Houdini's ability to create a moment of awe was its own kind of magic.

Chapter 4

The Great Mystery

"Real" magic, though, kept intruding on Houdini. The magic of spiritualism had become very popular. Spiritualists claimed they could talk with the spirits of the dead. When Houdini became disillusioned with this idea, he became spiritualism's greatest enemy. Perhaps this was because he had wanted so much for it to be true.

Many people had lost family members in World War I. They comforted themselves through "contacting" their dead loved ones. People called mediums helped them to do this. The mediums went into trances. Sometimes a bell would ring or a trumpet would sound. That meant a spirit was present. Sometimes the spirit would actually speak through the medium. The mediums claimed to be able to receive messages from spirits in the afterlife—and they usually charged a hefty fee for doing so. People who had lost someone they loved were glad to have those messages—and they paid the fees.

Houdini knew a lot about the tricks of spiritualism. When he worked with Dr. Hill's California Concert Company, he did tricks that looked like he contacted spirits. In his later act, he also did some "spirit magic." But he always admitted that what he did was just a trick.

Hocus-Pocus

Houdini enjoyed fooling people with "spirit magic." In 1914, he was returning to the United States from England. As he got ready for the voyage, he learned that former president Theodore Roosevelt would be on the same boat. The magician did some research on what Roosevelt had been doing recently. Then he prepared some special magic for the former president.

Houdini often did a magic show on a ship. This time, he asked members of his audience to write questions on pieces of paper. He gave several examples of the types of questions they might ask, and then he said he would answer their questions without reading the slips of paper!

Roosevelt wrote a question on a piece of paper. His question was folded and dropped between two blank chalkboard slates. Houdini took the slates and pretended to ask for spiritual aid. Then he opened the slates. The formerly blank surface of one slate now contained a multicolored map of South America. An arrow pointed to a river. On the other slate were the words, "Near the Andes." It was signed by a spirit who had gone down with the *Titanic* two years before.

Teddy Roosevelt's mouth hung open. The question he had written on his slip of paper was, "Where was I last Christmas?" The spirits had answered correctly! (And in color!)

Asked if the trick had been "real spiritualism," Houdini grinned at Roosevelt. "It was just hocus-pocus," he said.

Later Houdini told how he did this trick. He prepared the slates in advance and tried to plant the right question in Roosevelt's mind when he gave the examples of the kinds of questions to write. Then he handed the former president a book to write on. The book had carbon paper in it. It took only a second for Houdini to check the carbon and see if he'd gotten the right question. He had —and the trick worked.

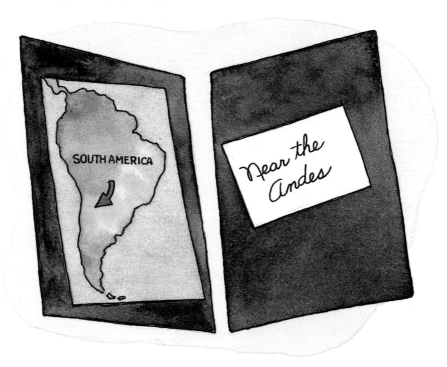

Willing to Believe

Yet, Houdini really did want to believe spiritualism was real. As a magician, Houdini had always wanted to "solve" the mystery of death. He called it "the great mystery." For years, Houdini had gone to seance after seance trying to contact his mother. His mother had tried to say something as she died, but had been unable to. Houdini thought she might have wanted to tell him to forgive his brother, Leopold, with whom Houdini had had a fight.

In England, Houdini met Sir Arthur Conan Doyle, the writer of the Sherlock Holmes stories. Doyle was a firm believer in spiritualism. In 1922, Doyle convinced Houdini to attend a seance with Doyle's wife, who was a medium. They would try to contact Houdini's mother, Cecilia.

Houdini attended the seance with hope in his heart. He longed to hear Cecilia's voice. He still missed her very much. And he was sure the Doyles would never deliberately fake anything.

The Seance

Seances usually took place around a table in a dark room. A medium led the meeting. Sometimes ghostly hands floated in the air. Trumpets appeared and played. Chains rattled. Bells rang. The spirits gave their messages through the voice or the writing of the medium.

Houdini sat with eyes closed in the darkness. "With a beating heart I waited, hoping that I might feel once more the presence of my beloved mother," he said later.

Sharp rapping noises made him open his eyes. Lady Doyle began to write. "At last I'm through. I've tried so often . . ." the medium wrote. "Now I am happy. . . . Why, of course, I want to talk to my boy . . . tell him I love him more than ever."

Houdini sat quietly as the medium wrote. He let her and the "spirit" finish. Then he left—silently and sadly.

The seance, Houdini believed, had not been real. The medium had written his mother's words in English.

Cecilia Weiss had known very little English. She had always spoken to Houdini in German. The day of the seance had also been Cecilia's birthday. Houdini thought it strange that her spirit hadn't mentioned the special day.

Houdini began to believe that no medium was real. He thought Lady Doyle was probably genuine in her belief, if not in her messages, but he thought that most mediums just used people's grief to make money. Houdini thought this was wrong, and so he set out to stop it.

Ghost Buster

Many people had investigated spiritualists. Doctors, scientists, and police had tried to figure out if what happened at seances was real or not. They found some fakes, but they also found some mediums who seemed genuine. They did things no one could explain. Houdini thought he could explain them. And if there was ever anyone qualified to catch a cheat, it was Houdini. He had conducted many seances for fun. He could also produce most "spirit magic" himself. If someone were using tricks, he would know.

Houdini went to many seances. He wore a false beard, wig, and thick glasses so he would not be recognized. When a trumpet played in the darkness, Houdini would flash on a light. The medium's helper would be caught with the trumpet to his lips. He was often covered by a black sheet so no one could see him.

Ripping off his disguise, Houdini would shout, "It is I—Houdini! You are a fraud!"

Of course, Houdini always made sure the reporters were there, along with the police, who would arrest the medium for fraud. He never forgot to use the magic of publicity.

The magician began to talk to his audiences about spiritualism during his magic show. He answered questions and showed how easily spirit magic could be faked. Houdini also challenged any medium to convince him that spirits were real. He said that he would pay $10,000 to anyone who could conjure up something he couldn't duplicate.

A Magician Among the Spirits

Soon Houdini was including his crusade against fake mediums in every stage show. He began with magic tricks. In the second part of the show, he concentrated on escapes. Then he would invite members of the audience up onto the stage for a seance. They would be blindfolded to simulate the darkened room of a seance. Then Houdini would summon the "spirits." He showed how mediums could write on slates with their toes. He reproduced the floating hands that often brushed participants' faces during seances. (They were simply gloves coated with white paint that glowed in the dark. The gloves were then glued to black cardboard. In the dark, they appeared to hang in the air.)

Houdini also showed how a medium would make a megaphone seem to fly across a room or crash to the floor. This was a common gimmick used by mediums. The medium would simply put a megaphone on her head in the dark, before joining hands with the people around the table. Then, she would take their hands and—snap! She used her neck to toss the megaphone.

People loved Houdini's show more than ever. Houdini even wrote a book, *A Magician Among the Spirits*, explaining how he exposed the fake mediums. Not one medium collected the $10,000 Houdini offered. "I contend from this," Houdini said, "nobody can get communication from the dead."

Death Pacts

Deep down, though, Houdini was disappointed by his failure to find even one genuine medium. He still wanted to contact his mother. He didn't want to believe it was impossible to speak to the dead. But he was angered by people who pretended that their tricks were more than illusions. He especially disliked fake mediums who took money for their seances.

But Houdini wanted to believe, and he held the hope that perhaps he would be the one to overcome death. After all, he had solved many puzzles during his lifetime. Why not this one?

Houdini began to make death pacts with his friends. He made fourteen of them. Those who died were to try desperately to reach those who still lived. When Houdini's secretary, John William Sargent, died, Houdini waited to hear from him. No word came. Others who had made pacts died. Houdini waited. Still no word came.

Houdini made one final death pact—with Bess. They set up a secret coded message. Houdini would try to give Bess a message in code after his death if he could. She was to hold a seance on the anniversary of his death and wait for him to contact her. If she died first, Bess would do

the same. The code was one they had used together during their circus days. No one else knew it.

Doomed, Doomed, Doomed!

Houdini had always thought a lot about death. He had never gotten over his mother's death. And now there was a steady stream of predictions of his own death. In 1924, a famous spiritualist named Margery the Medium said that Houdini had less than a year to live. Her prediction didn't come true, but many mediums, who disliked what Houdini did to their careers, put hexes on him. Even Sir Arthur Conan Doyle received a message from a medium in England: "Houdini is doomed, doomed, doomed!"

Houdini grew irritated by these threats. He said that if he died, it would be because it was God's will, not some medium's. But Houdini knew he had many enemies because of his crusade against spiritualism. He began to use bodyguards. Friends reported that he was haunted by thoughts of his own death. When he left his home in New York in October of 1926, he made the driver go back so he could look at his house once more. He believed he would never see it again.

Chapter 5

Last Challenge

When Houdini began his last tour, it seemed at first that it was Bess's life that was threatened. Houdini was performing in Rhode Island when Bess awoke one morning seriously ill. The doctors said it was ptomaine poisoning. Houdini was frantic. Bess was the most important thing in his life. Houdini worked during the days and sat by Bess's side through the nights. When they moved on to Albany, New York, Houdini hadn't slept for three nights in a row.

An Accident

Though Houdini was tired and worried, he didn't let it affect his performance. Everything was going fine during the first performance in Albany—until the Chinese Water Torture Cell Escape. Houdini's helpers locked the stocks around Houdini's ankles. Ropes jerked him, upside down, into the air. Suddenly Houdini shouted for the rope-pullers to stop. Something was wrong.

A doctor from the audience rushed to the stage to examine the magician. He told Houdini to go to a hospital for an x-ray. Houdini's ankle had probably been broken when he was jerked into the air. Houdini said he would go to the hospital—after the show. The audience cheered him on.

Houdini didn't do the water-cell escape, but he did finish the rest of the show. Then he went to the hospital. His ankle was broken. The newspapers predicted that Houdini would be off the stage for a while. They did not know Harry Houdini! He didn't miss a performance.

A Sudden Punch

Houdini finished his performances in Albany and moved on to Montreal, Ontario. Bess was still ill, but she was a little better, and so she came along on the long trip. In Montreal, Houdini spoke to some students about spirit fraud. During his speech, one of the students sketched the magician. Houdini saw the drawing and liked the student's work. He invited the student to the theater to do a close-up portrait later in the week.

On Friday, October 22, 1926, the student returned to sketch Houdini. While he drew, there was a knock on the dressing room door. Another student, J. Gordon Whitehead, had come to return a book he had borrowed from the magician.

Whitehead asked if it was true that anyone could punch Houdini in the stomach without it hurting him. Houdini

said yes, without really paying much attention to the young man. He was resting his injured ankle on a couch and reading his mail. When Whitehead asked if he could "throw a punch" at Houdini, Houdini mumbled, "Sure."

Without warning, the student swung. He punched Houdini hard in the stomach! Houdini's face went white. "I wasn't set," he gasped.

After he caught his breath, Houdini stood up and set his muscles. This time, Whitehead's fist felt as if it hit a solid wall. But the damage had been done.

After a while, the students left. Houdini went on reading his mail. Later that afternoon, Houdini felt some pain in his abdomen. By evening, the pain had become intense. Still, Houdini thought it was just a torn muscle.

Bess, who was still weak herself, begged him to see a doctor. Houdini refused. The training for his escape acts had given him the ability to withstand a lot of pain. Besides, he had a show to do!

By the end of the Montreal show on October 23, Houdini had a temperature of 102 degrees. He still insisted on helping to pack the stage props. Then he boarded the overnight train to Detroit for his next show.

Finally, on the train, he couldn't stand the pain any longer. An assistant wired ahead for a doctor to meet the train. When they arrived in Detroit on the morning of October 24, the doctor told Houdini he had appendicitis. He must go to a hospital immediately.

Houdini went on stage instead. The theater was full. "They're here to see me," Houdini said. "I won't disappoint them."

The Last Show

The audience stomped and clapped as they waited for the show to begin. At last, Houdini walked on to the stage. He was smiling and full of tricks. Silver coins vanished from his fingertips. They dropped into a hanging glass box all by themselves! Alarm clocks disappeared from Houdini's hands—and appeared, ringing, at the other end of the stage. A pretty young woman, somehow, turned into a flower bush.

A spectator tossed Houdini a deck of cards. He chal-

lenged the great magician to do tricks with an unfamiliar deck. Houdini did so easily. The audience roared.

Houdini defied the mediums of Detroit. He exposed their tricks. He answered questions asked by members of the audience.

Houdini did his entire show. Only Bess and his helpers knew that Houdini was in trouble; every move was painful. When the curtains closed, Houdini collapsed. His temperature was now 104 degrees. His appendix had burst.

The Broken Wand

That afternoon, doctors removed Houdini's appendix. His condition was grave. The doctors didn't expect him to live for more than twelve hours.

For a while, Houdini held on. He was fighting his last challenge—death. Bess had collapsed, from her own illness as well as from worry about Houdini. However, she still spent as much time as she could with her husband.

Several days later Houdini was still alive, but doctors had to operate again. Newspapers kept Houdini's fans informed of his condition.

On October 29, Houdini called for Bess and reminded her of the word he would try to communicate from the grave. It would be in code. That way Bess would be able to tell if the message was really from him.

On Sunday, October 31, Houdini knew there would be no escape from this challenge. "I guess this thing is going to get me," he told his brother, Theo. Bess hugged him.

Then, the Great Houdini, the Handcuff King, Champion Jail Breaker, and Supreme Ruler of Magic closed his eyes and died. He was 52 years old. It was Halloween.

After Houdini's last show in Detroit, all his props had been packed up and sent back to his home in New York. Strangely, a bronze casket he planned to use in his escape act had been left behind. No one knew why. That casket carried Houdini's body back to New York. There, he was buried beside his mother.

At the funeral, The Society of American Magicians broke a magician's wand over the casket. They chanted: "The curtain has been rung down. The wand is broken."

The Pact

Bess kept her part of the pact she and Houdini had made. Every Halloween, on the anniversary of her husband's death, she visited mediums and held seances, always waiting for the message Houdini had said he would send. Bess offered a reward to anyone who could prove he had been in contact with Houdini. She kept a light shining in front of Houdini's picture day and night.

Many mediums contacted her, saying they had a message from Houdini, but none of the messages was the one Houdini had said he would send. Bess had to conclude they were all fakes. Then, in 1928, Bess received a message from a spiritualist named Arthur Ford. Houdini's mother had contacted him, he said. She needed to give a message to open the door for Houdini to communicate with Bess. Her message was, "forgive."

Bess was amazed. That was the message Houdini had expected to hear from his mother all those years! She sent a notice to the press saying that only she and Houdini had known that message, forgetting that she had told a newspaper reporter a few months earlier.

Bess waited for Ford to get a message from Houdini. Ford held seances for almost a year. For the first nine months, nothing happened. Then the word "Rosabelle"

came through. Rosabelle was Houdini's pet name for Bess. Over the next couple months other words came: Rosabelle . . . answer . . . tell . . . pray . . . answer . . . look . . . tell . . . answer . . . answer . . . tell. When he was sure he had the right words in the right order, Ford went to Bess with the message. It was the code she and Houdini had used for their mind-reading act during their circus days!

Each word represented a number from one to ten. The numbers could be combined to give the position of any letter in the alphabet. For example, "pray" was the number one and "answer" was the number two, so "pray answer" was the number twelve, which stood for the letter "L." When decoded, Houdini's message read, "Believe"—the word Houdini had promised to send Bess from the grave!

Bess believed. The story flashed around the world. But Houdini's brother Theo worried that Bess was being tricked. He reminded Bess of the newspaper story that told of Houdini's mother and the message "forgive." And he reminded her that the pact she and Houdini had made was no longer a secret, either. A biography of Houdini had described it in detail. Bess herself had told the story to the biographer. Slowly, with Theo's help, Bess began to doubt that the message had really come from her husband.

Yet, Bess still wondered if Houdini had been trying to break through. She kept the light burning by his picture and held seances on the anniversary of his death for ten years.

HOUDINI AND BESS'S CODE

pray—1
answer—2
say—3
now—4
tell—5
please—6
speak—7
quickly—8
look—9
be quick—10

MESSAGE HOUDINI PROMISED

answer—B
tell—E
pray answer—L
look—I
tell—E
answer answer—V
tell—E

"Good night, Harry"

Finally, Bess planned one last seance. It was to be held on Halloween, the tenth anniversary of Houdini's death. Houdini's brother Theo attended the seance. Bess's friend, Edward Saint, called for the great magician's spirit to come to them. He asked Houdini to open the locked handcuffs on the table. He could even just ring a bell or shake a tambourine.

Nothing happened.

Dr. Saint asked Bess what to do. Sadly, she said, "I do not believe that Houdini can come back to me or to anyone. . . . The light has burned for ten years. I now regretfully turn out the light. This is the end. Good night, Harry!"

As Bess, Theo, and Dr. Saint left the seance, they heard a low rumble of thunder. The sky filled with clouds, and it started to rain—just enough to get everyone wet. Some people said *that* was how the Great Houdini sent a message!

(courtesy Historical Pictures Service, Chicago)

Man of Mystery

Bess died in 1943. Houdini's 5000 books on magic went to the Library of Congress in Washington, D.C. His tricks, locks, and handcuffs were given to his brother Theo and various friends.

Mysteriously, though, the ghost of Houdini still haunts us. Seances are held for Houdini nearly every Halloween by his loyal fans. There are rumors that his riches still exist in a bank vault under a fake name. Others believe that a box filled with his secrets will appear on Halloween a hundred years after his death—2026. Some people even claim to have seen Houdini's ghost. They say it lives in the Palace Theatre in New York.

So far, none of these stories has been proven true—or false. The mysteries remain, and with good reason. Harry Houdini, the man of mystery, would have wanted it that way!

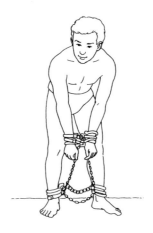

Chapter 6

The Mystery of Magic

Houdini was a man of mystery and even today his magic remains mysterious. Everyone who ever sat in Houdini's audience was struck with wonder. How could he escape from those chains, and trunks, and crates? How could he saw a woman into pieces and then put her back together again? How could he make a coin, or a flower, or an elephant disappear? Inevitably, the question came up: was it all just a trick, or was Houdini performing real magic?

Gold from Iron

Throughout history, there have been those who have taken magic seriously. The Druids of ancient Britain cast spells. Nearly every village in medieval Europe had a "wise woman" who could make a love potion, cure disease, and foresee the future. Alchemists sought a magical means to turn base metals into gold. Famous scholars of the sixteenth and seventeenth centuries wrote books on magical ritual. Even in today's world, there are those who believe that real magic exists.

A Psychic Force

Throughout his life, Houdini himself questioned whether real magic existed. He sought out the other great magicians of his time, asking whether they had ever experienced some sort of supernatural power. Houdini knew that many magicians through the years believed that if they performed certain actions perfectly and recited just the right words perfectly, magic would occur. They called this a magic ritual. Houdini wondered if a magical trick might not become a magical ritual. If the trick were performed over and over again until it was "perfect," couldn't it release some psychic force, a supernatural energy, which really made magic happen?

Houdini wondered all this because he sometimes felt as if he hadn't actually done a trick, but rather that something supernatural had happened. Sometimes, when he performed his escapes so fast, he felt as if he did actually leave his body. And sometimes, when faced with a difficult lock, it seemed the prayer he breathed was more responsible for the lock opening than his pick. Could it really be magic? Or did it just seem so?

There have been many great magicians who have performed amazing magic on the stage. But none of them has claimed that he had supernatural powers which enabled him to perform his tricks. Before Houdini, Robert-Houdin made his son float in the air. Herrmann the Great cut a man's head off, sat it on a cabinet, and listened to the head talk. Harry Kellar made a mechanical robot shake hands, spell, do arithmetic problems, play cards, and smoke cigarettes—all without the robot being attached to any power source. And Howard Thurston called a man up on stage and removed animals from his jacket.

These men and others like them created great marvels for their audiences to wonder at. But they always said anyone could perform their tricks—if they knew the secrets. Every time Houdini was able to talk magic with another magician, he always got that same answer. They did not tap any psychic force to do their tricks, and they had never seen anyone convincingly demonstrate real supernatural powers.

In his head, Houdini was convinced that supernatural powers could not exist; but in his heart, there was always a seed of doubt—and others shared that doubt.

(courtesy Historical Pictures Service, Chicago)

Magical Energy

People who saw Houdini's act often believed he must have supernatural powers. James Hewat Mackenzie, president of the Psychic College, believed it. Mackenzie was once a member of the committee Houdini called up from the audience during his act. The committee was supposed to inspect all the props and keep an eye on things, so that no "trickery" could be used. Mackenzie stood on the stage while Houdini escaped from the Chinese Water Torture Cell. As Houdini escaped, Mackenzie suddenly felt weak and drained. Mackenzie said he recognized that

feeling. He had felt it before—during seances where spirits appeared. It seemed that spirits needed to draw psychic energy from the living in order to materialize. Mackenzie said that whether Houdini knew it or not, he was drawing psychic energy from his audience committees in order to perform his escapes.

Sir Arthur Conan Doyle agreed. Throughout his life, Doyle was convinced that Houdini fought so hard against mediums because he was hiding from the fact that he was himself a very powerful medium.

Sarah Bernhardt

Even the great actress Sarah Bernhardt thought Houdini might have supernatural powers.

In 1917 Madame Bernhardt witnessed one of Houdini's "hanging from a building straitjacket escapes" in Boston. Afterward, she called Houdini and Bess to her car and invited them for a ride. Three years before, Madame Bernhardt had had one of her legs amputated. During the car ride, she put her arm around Houdini and asked, "Houdini, you do such marvelous things. Couldn't you—could you bring back my leg for me?" With deep regret, Houdini had to tell her no.

Proof

Many people have offered large sums of money to anyone who can produce genuine supernatural phenomenon under controlled circumstances. No one has been able to collect that money. People have tried, but the magic that they do—flying, moving objects, reading people's minds—can all be duplicated by stage magicians through tricks of one sort or another. That doesn't mean those people necessarily used trickery, but science will only accept a supernatural explanation for something if no natural explanation will work.

There are some things science hasn't explained. UFO sightings, poltergeist, E.S.P., and Bigfoot are a few of the mysteries science hasn't been able to account for. Scientists say they merely have to continue to look for explanations. They are sure everything can be explained without having to resort to the supernatural. And many people who claim to have supernatural powers have been shown to be either lying or fooling themselves because they want so much to believe.

Since Houdini's death, other great magicians have emerged. Harry Blackstone, The Great Cardini (who took his name from "card" and "Houdini"), Joseph Dunniger, and Milbourne Christopher have all astounded audiences. Two young magicians, Doug Henning and David Copperfield, stand in the magic spotlight today. But none of them lays claim to supernatural powers.

(courtesy AP/Wide World Photos)

Perhaps there are no such powers. Perhaps science is right that an explanation can always be found sooner or later. Perhaps, but perhaps not. It could be that science has too limted a view.

Houdini performed wondrous magic. Audiences who saw him marveled at his skill. Was it all just trickery, or was there something a little supernatural about it all? That's the Great Mystery!

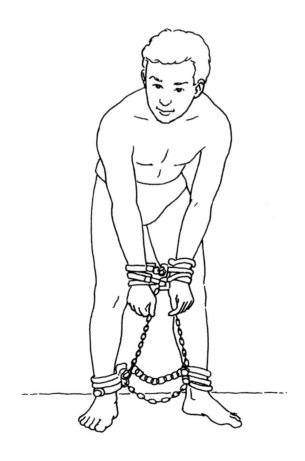

INDEX

Albany, New York, 71-72
Appleton, Wisconsin, 11, 13
Berlin, Germany, 36
Bernhardt, Sarah, 96
Blackstone, Harry, 97
brick wall illusion, 50, 53
Chicago, Illinois, 27-28
Chicago Journal, 28
Chicago World's Fair, 16, 19
Chinese Water Torture Cell, 36, 71-72, 94
Christopher, Milbourne, 97
Columbia Theater, 35
Copperfield, David, 97
Daily Illustrated Mirror, 40
Detroit, Michigan, 75, 77, 79
Doctor Hill's California Concert Company, 19-20, 56
Doyle, Sir Arthur Conan, 59-61, 69, 95
Dunniger, 97
Ford, Arthur, 80-82
Garfield, James A., 32
Great Cardini, The, 97
Great Cirnoc, 30-31
Guiteau, Charles, 32
handcuff escapes, 11, 27, 28-31, 40-41, 43
Henning, Doug, 97
Herrmann the Great, 92
Hill, Dr., 19-21
Houdini, Bess, 19, 21, 25, 40-41, 46, 48, 66, 71-72, 74, 77-87
Hyman, Jacob, 15
Jack Hoefler's Five Cent Circus, 13
jail escapes, 11, 27-33
Jennie the elephant, 45-46
Kansas City Post, 38
Kellar, Harry, 92
Liberty, Miss, 49
London, England, 28, 30, 40
Los Angeles, California, 27
Mackenzie, James Hewat, 94-95

Magician Among the Spirits, A, 66
Margery the Medium, 69
Melbourne, Australia, 31
Metamorphosis, 16
Milk Can, The, 35
Montreal, Ontario, 72
Needles, 46
Palace Theater, 87
Philadelphia, Pennsylvania, 27
Robert-Houdin, Jean-Eugene, 15, 92
Roosevelt, Theodore, 56-58
Saint, Dr. Edward, 84-85
St. Louis, Missouri, 35
Sargent, John William, 66
Scotland Yard, 28
Society of American Magicians, The, 79
spiritualism, 21-22, 55-69
straitjacket escapes, 38
Thurston, Howard, 92
Titanic, 56
Weiss, Cecilia, 11, 13, 38, 59-61
Weiss, Leopold, 59
Weiss, Samuel, 11
Weiss, Theo, 14, 16, 19, 79, 82, 84-85, 87
Whitehead, J. Gordon, 72, 74